The Middle Child

AF244191

By

Shaunice Henry

Hi, I am
Shaunice
Henry, the
middle kid of
my family of
six my mom,

dad and my
two sisters
and one
brother. This is
my story of my

life as the middle kid. When you are a middle child, you no longer fit in your

family,
because you
are not the
oldest and you
are not the
baby you

simply just
doesn't have a
role in the
family so you
are just left
out.

Let us start from the beginning first; you have my big sister Kaycee

She is mean but she can also be funny and outgoing sometimes. I love spending time with her. However, she always get away from cleaning and doing things

around the house.
Then you have me (Shauny)
I am very shy but I can be

funny, and I
also can be full
of myself
being
That I am
trying to be

number one
well, I always
try my best to
be. I feel
lonely
sometimes

being the
middle child.
The middle
child also has
its up's and
down like

being able to have good relationships with both siblings the older and younger siblings. I try to keep the peace between all of us because it

can get out of
control
sometimes
between
siblings.

Next there's
my other
sister Sophia,
She is mostly
happy but can

tend to have a terrible attitude with me at times. She also gets away with

many things
being that she
is treated like
the baby girl
of our family.

Last is my baby brother Anthony. He is very funny but he is just like my baby sister

(Sophia). He tends to have a very bad attitude at times. He is also the baby

and never
seems to find
himself in
trouble
because he is
the "baby"

and since

there's

an even

number of

four children

that means

there are two
middle kids
Sophia and I,
but I feel more
like the middle
child because,

I am always blamed; about different stuff and I am always getting treated mean

by my siblings.
I always find
myself getting
into trouble
because the
other children

just gets away with everything! Now that we are done with that. Let us talk about some life experiences I have being through as a middle kid, and how it feels to be the middle kid. First we can talk about the time my

family went to
Canada we
were going
out to eat I ask
for a milk
shake and I

was told "no"
and my baby
brother
"asked for
something"
and he got it,

let us guess just because he's the baby right! How fair is that? Then there's

all those times
where I'm told
to 'clean up
'when the rest
of my

Siblings are in their rooms playing games, either reading, or sleeping.

These some experiences that middle kids have to go through in life.

It is my
opinion that
the middle kid
is always the
odd child; well
it seems that

way growing up. However, we middle kids do have one day per year to celebrate

and its August
12 middle
child day.

This is my life as a middle kid.

The End.